From

MW00941989

Power

30-Day Devotional for
Strength within the Process

CG Mclean Jr.

4-U-Nique
Publishing

Breaking the Status Quo, One Book at a Time.™

4-U-Nique Publishing
A Series of VLB/VBJ Enterprises, LLC

4-U-Nique Publishing books may be purchased for educational,
business, or sales promotional use. For information, please email:
info@4-U-Nique Publishing.com

First Edition

Cover Design By: 4-U-Nique Publishing

Library of Congress Cataloging-in-Publication Data

ISBN-13: 9781677217670

Preface

Often in life, we go through things that cause us to feel a great deal of pain. We may not understand exactly why we have to experience and deal with these situations. This 30-day devotional is not a book to guarantee you find the answers to why you are experiencing these painful situations. This devotional is a 30-day guide to usher you in the presence of God so that in his presence you can grow through whatever it is you are going through. It's not a book to remove your problems but it will help you understand that God will insert himself when you invite him in your situations. From Pain to Power 30-day devotional is centered on 2 Corinthians 12:9, "My grace is sufficient for you, for my power is made perfect in weakness." So if you are in this space, this is the book for you. Enjoy!

Day 1

Scripture

Philippians 4:6-7

(6) Do not be anxious about anything, but in every situation, by prayer and petition, with thanksgiving, present your request to God (7) and the peace of God, which transcends all understanding, will guard your hearts and your minds in Christ Jesus.

Thought

The pain that you feel has a way of creating anxiety and hopelessness. If you aren't careful, staying in a place of pain can rob you of the peace and purpose that God has for you. Feelings of anxiety, depression, and regret are all warning signs that should lead you to the throne of God and prayer. When you pray and make your request known to God, he will grant you the peace you need even in the midst of your storms and trials. God will allow you to go through circumstances without those circumstances going through you. Your *faith* and your *strength* are being developed **NOT** destroyed.

Practice

For the next 30 days, I want you to pray every morning before getting your day started. Pray to God about the source of your pain with the belief that God will do exactly what he said he would do. Then spend 15 minutes in the morning and night meditating on Philippians 4:6-7. Write down what you believe God to do for you.

Day 2

Scripture

Corinthians 12:9

And he has said unto me, "My grace is sufficient for you, for power is perfected in weakness." Most gladly therefore, I will rather boast about my weaknesses, so that the power of Christ may dwell in me.

Thought

In a world where we are taught only the strong survive, we are surrounded by people who boast in the power of their strength. Many feel like they've created all they have and made it as far as they have by their own doing. However, when you face situations that bring you more problems and pain than you can bear, it is important to know who is the source of your strength and the strength of your life.

When you can admit your weaknesses, you then can experience the outpour of God's love, joy, peace, happiness, comfort, strength and more. However, it is up to you to invite God into every situation and every aspect of your life.

Practice

For the next 29 days during your prayer time tell God your weaknesses and ask him to fill you wherever you feel a void. Also, before you go to bed tonight, write down the names of God. Sometimes in life, the overflow experience may not be that your cup runs over. Nevertheless, it is still an amazing blessing to know that while it might not run over, God will not let your cup run out.

Day 3

Scripture

1 John 4:4

Greater is He that is in you, than he that is in the world.

Thought

Regardless of what you face and are up against, you are made in God's image. The Holy Spirit that dwells within you is **greater**, **bigger**, and **larger** than that which is in the world. The pain, the hurt, and the discomfort will not take you out. You serve a God who is bigger, wiser, and stronger.

Practice

For the next 28 days, find 2 or 3 songs that speak to you. Listen to the songs throughout the day, learn the words, and sing them over and over out loud for the next 28 days. Faith comes by hearing the Word of God. You want to feed your spirit the nutrients it needs to *POWER UP* beyond the pain.

Day 4

Scripture

Romans 8: 38-39

(38) For I am persuaded, that neither death, nor life, nor angels, nor principalities, nor powers, nor things present, nor things to come, (39) Nor height, nor depth, nor any other creatures, shall be able to separate from the love of God, which is in Christ Jesus our Lord.

Thought

Often we can go through situations and look at it as if God is trying to punish us for our sins, our shortcomings, or our past. This is not to say that our decisions will not have consequences that we must face. However, what is being conveyed is, that regardless of *ANYTHING* that you may be facing, God loves you. God always has and always will love you. It is the Lord's love that is perfect, pure, and it is only *HIS LOVE* that *STRENGTHENS US*. Remember, there is *NOTHING* that can separate you from the *LOVE* of God.

Practice

For the next 27 days, at least 10 times a day, remind yourself that there is nothing that can separate you from the *LOVE* of God. Write it, sing it, draw it, shout it, speak it, paint it, and GET IT engraved into your mind and heart, *GOD LOVES YOU AND THERE IS NOTHING IN THIS WORLD THAT CAN SEPARATE YOU FROM HIS LOVE.*

Day 5

Scripture

Psalm 107:1

"Give thanks to the LORD, for he is good; his love endures forever."

1 Thessalonians 5:18 (NIV)

"Give thanks in all circumstances, for this is God's will for you in Christ Jesus.

Thought

The best weapon against the spirit of despair (helplessness) is your praise. Having a spirit of praise, gratefulness, and thanksgiving will help transition your perspective of the situation you are facing in life. Having a spirit of praise will jump-start the power you desire and cause a paradigm shift that will jolt you into the position to receive the blessings God has for you.

Practice

Today, make it a point to have hour praise and worship service with just you and God. Read scriptures on God's power and praise. After reading 3 to 5 scriptures, play some good praise and worship music and press into the presence of God. You may not be in the mood and you could have 1000 reasons not to, but remember God loves you and there is nothing that can separate you from his love. Dig in deep and just let the Spirit lead you in that hour. After the hour ends, I challenge you to write a list of things that you thank God for. I want you to do this at least once every day for the next 5 days.

Day 6

Scripture

John 14:27

I am leaving you with a gift- peace of mind and hear. And the peace I give is a gift the world cannot give. So don't be troubled or afraid.

Thought

The world's view of peace and tranquility is a quiet stillness void of any troubles, complications, or tests. This is not only a misconception and false interpretation of peace, but it is also unrealistic. Peace is being in the midst of trials and tribulations and still being calm at heart, while having confidence that God is in control of it all. To have peace in the middle of your pain, it is imperative to recognize who is the prince of peace and relinquish all control to him. It's easy to feel as though we have to figure everything out on our own. This feeling is what will rob you of your peace of mind and heart faster than anything else. You are not in control; God is.

Practice

Today, I need you to confess that you are giving all of your worries, cares, troubles and, fears to God. Write, "God is in control of everything", on a sheet of paper 137 times. Place it somewhere you can see over the next 25 days.

Day 7

Scripture

Psalm 27:1

The Lord is my light and my salvation; whom shall I fear? The Lord is the strength of my life; of whom shall I be afraid?

Thought

Life has a way of making us feel like we are surrounded by darkness and that the pain will overcome us and be the determining factor in our demise. It is important to remember that God is our light and salvation. Light penetrates through darkness. Once the darkness is penetrated, we also have to know that our Lord will save us from dangers seen and unseen. Knowing this will keep us from staying in darkness and it will protect us from staying in a place of despair and defeat.

When you realize that God is the strength of your life, you will understand that while your life is not void of issues, God has given you everything that you need to not only make it through situations and circumstances but to GROW THROUGH them. You will come to find out that you can go through the tough situations of life without them overcoming you.

Practice

Learn what the full armor of God is and make sure that you put them on every day for the next 24 days, before leaving the house and getting engulfed with your daily activities. The helmet of Salvation, the shield of Faith, the breastplate of righteousness, the belt of Truth, the sword of the spirit, and the Gospel of Peace. While these things make up the full armor of God, they don't exactly tell you what each of the components is used for. I challenge you to research and pray on each of the components of the full armor to give you an understanding of what they are used for.

Day 8

Scripture

Isaiah 54:17

No weapon formed against thee shall prosper, and every tongue that shall rise against thee in judgement thou shalt condemn. This is the heritage of the servants of the LORD, and their righteousness is of me, says the LORD.

Thought

Living a life with Jesus at the forefront is a life of victory. As a member in the body of Christ with Jesus at the head, we don't have to fight for the victory; we can fight from the victory. Jesus won the victory when we were yet sinners. Knowing that he died on the cross for our sins allows us to defeat any weapon that forms against us. Because of his resurrection we are made righteous with belief in what he did for us many years ago. It's your legacy.

Practice

For the next 23 days, anytime you start to feel attacked or feel weapons forming to distract, stop or defeat you, say no weapon formed against me shall prosper. Say it as many times as you need to.

Day 9

Scripture

2 Samuel 22:33

God is my strength and my power: and he maketh my way perfect.

Thought

When you commune with God you will see that he will become your strength to endure and your power to overcome. When you stop and listen to his voice you will get a play by play, step by step direction that makes your way perfect. While it may not seem like things are making sense and nothing is going the way you would hope. You have to understand, it's not about disciplining you, as much as it is about developing you into what he has called you to be. Like an athlete who stays in constant communication with a coach. Just as your GPS directs you, you will see God direct your path once you take the steps to stay in constant communication with your coach.

Practice

Stand in the mirror and state, "God is my strength and my power: and he makes my way perfect." Say it as many times as you need until you start to feel empowered by the Holy Spirit.

Day 10

Scripture

Proverbs 18:20

Words satisfy the souls as food satisfies the stomach; the right words on a person's lips bring satisfaction.

Thought

"As a man thinks in his heart so is he, and it is out of the abundance of the heart that the mouth speaks." Often how we see ourselves and what we say about ourselves show us just how much we value ourselves. Often when we go through situations, we speak what we are going through and the mistakes that we have made as if it is who we are. Regardless of what we are going through and regardless of the mistakes that we make, we need to affirm what God has told us and said about us so we can value ourselves in the same manner God sees us.

Practice

Pray that God gives you the words to affirm the way that he sees you. As they come to you, write them down.

Day 11

Scripture

Psalms 46:10

Be still and know that I am God.

Thought

When we feel as though we are going through tough times, pain, troubles and or just everyday struggles, we have a tendency to try to make things happen on our own. We run ourselves rampant trying to solve all of our perceived issues and problems. Once we come to our wits end is when we can just **STOP** and **RELY** on God to work things out in our favor as believers. You can search high and low, and not find anyone who can do what God can do. Sometimes, in order for God to move, he is waiting on you to be still and let him get into his position.

25

Practice

Pray that God continues to give you words to affirm you and allow you to see yourself as God sees you. Continue to write them down.

DAY 12

Scripture

Proverbs 18:21

The tongue has the power of life and death, and those who love it will eat its fruit.

Thought

A lot of times we will speak against the very thing we have been praying and believing for out of frustration. It's important to discipline our tongue to speak life when and where it's necessary. **Only** speak death to those things we are directed to speak death to. When you can see things coming up against what you are hoping and believing for then it is ok to speak to death to them, as Jesus cursed the fig tree that was bare of fruit. When the thing you are believing for doesn't look like you feel it should, it is important not to speak out of frustration but to speak life from the faith that lives inside of you. The toughest thing to do is speak life over ourselves and situations when we don't feel like it. This is where affirmations and promises come into play. We have to intentionally speak life over ourselves.

Practice

Over the next 19 days, in the morning and at night, take the list of affirmations you comprised over the last 2 days and speak them over yourself.

Day 13

Scripture

Psalm 51:17

My sacrifice, O God, is a broken spirit, a broken and contrite heart you, God will not despise.

Thought

Often we go through life feeling and thinking more of ourselves than we really are. Once we get too engulfed on our high horse life has a way of knocking us down. When we reach the moment of getting knocked down, our response to the situation and circumstance can either take us into the presence of God or further into despair. If we humble ourselves and run to the father from which comes our help he will supply us with everything that we are in need of. Regardless, if you caused the pain you are going through, someone else did or it's just something God is allowing, he will not shun or reject you.

Practice

Listen to these 2 songs at some point in the day

Gracefully broken by Tasha Cobbs

Joy by VaShawn Mitchell

Day 14

Scripture

Jeremiah 10:6

No one is like you, LORD; you are great, and your name is mighty in power.

Thought

Many times when we feel the most pain in our lives it is because we are looking at our situation and circumstances through magnifying our issues and looking at what the opposition is as an unstoppable an unbeatable Goliath of sorts. One thing we have to remember is that Goliath eventually fell. Just as David was able to overcome Goliath, the giants that you face in life, I don't care how big or how many they are, they aren't nearly as great, mighty or powerful as the God you serve. In order to turn your pain into power you have to change your perspective. Your God is bigger than your situations. That's not some religious rhetoric that is **The Honest To God Truth.**

Practice

Sometimes, it takes times of reflection to change our perspective. Make time to write down how many ways God has shown how great he has been in your life.

Day 15

Scripture

1 Thessalonians 5:18

In everything give thanks; for this is the will of God in Christ Jesus for you.

Thought

The absolute best weapon we have is the weapon of praise and worship. Let's dispel the myth now, praise isn't a song, it's a posture of obedience and gratefulness. Both are rooted in a spirit of thanksgiving. This is a discipline that has to be intentionally and purposefully done. When life isn't lined up the way we desire and things aren't going our way we have to praise God, **No Matter the Circumstance or Situation**. The best way to give thanks in the middle of a storm is to remind yourself of all the storms God got you through before this. He has done it for you before. God who is the same yesterday today and forevermore he will do it for you again.

Practice

Take time to look over the list that you wrote yesterday. Play some worship music and intentionally give him thanks for those things that he has done for you in the past. Let him know, not only do you thank him, but you trust and love him.

Day 16

Scripture

Matthew 6:5-6

"And when you pray, do not be like the hypocrites, for they love to pray standing in the synagogues and on the street corners to be seen by others. Truly I tell you, they have received their reward in full. But when you pray, go into your room, close the door and pray to your Father, who is unseen.

Thought

Having a prayer group is awesome! Praying for people will also give you strength. One-on-one time with God in your own secret place is rewarding beyond description. Having a place that is dedicated to prayer is like building an altar where you will go and talk to the Lord and spend quality time with him. It's like having a go to place with your significant other. No matter the state of your relationship, when you all go to a designated place it lends a level of peace to you. A secret sacred place for you to pour your heart out to God will lead to peace in the middle of a storm and will give you **POWER** in the midst of your **PAIN**.

Practice

Set up a place of prayer somewhere in your living quarters. Put scriptures up, affirmations, pictures, and anything else you would want to set your atmosphere the way you'd like. Bring pen and paper to write down what the Lord says to you. Before leaving your prayer closet pray over it. Going forward, make your morning and night prayers in this space.

Day 17

Scripture

1 Thessalonians 5:17

Pray without ceasing.

Thought

There are times when we pray and we can feel refreshed and filled with what we need, which is not a bad thing. The issue comes when we think we are good and can handle the situations of life with that one filling. You have to look at your physical body and know that you have to eat, drink, and sleep consistently or you will experience a shutdown or a breakdown that's detrimental to your health. To obtain spiritual wellness you have to consistently meditate, read the word, fast, and pray. These are the disciplines that are needed in order to ensure you are spiritually fit to fight the battles that we as believers face in life.

Practice

Take time to go to your prayer closet and pray specifically about the things that have been the focal points of your pain. Stay in their as long as you feel. I challenge you to be as transparent, authentic, and real as possible.

Day 18

Scripture

Psalm 16:8

I have set the Lord always before me. Because he is at my right hand, will not be shaken.

Thought

When you know the Lord and the position he holds in your life it will become easier to face the trials in life. You will go through things without them going through you. Where are your eyes set? What are you focused on? Don't focus on your pain or your problems. Focus on your God. Do you know who your God is? Do you know everything he is capable of? That should be a refreshing thought. That should fill you with a supernatural confidence.

Practice

Take a pen and paper and list in order everything that has your focus from greatest to least amount of focus. If your list doesn't have God, your Lord and Savior as number 1 priority in your life, there is you're most pressing need. Do whatever you can to make sure your eyes are set on him.

Day 19

Scripture

Hebrews 12:2

Looking unto Jesus the author and finisher of our faith; who for the joy that was set before him endured the cross, despising the shame, and is set.

Thought

Sometimes when we are focused on Jesus, we don't think of the fact that he has finished the work for us when he died on the cross for our sins. We have to know that we already have the victory. We aren't fighting for the victory but from the victory. There are things we must face and endure with victory so others can see the **Victory of Christ** in our life. You are victorious, you are an overcomer. There is a crown for you. However, you must hold on to your cross and follow Jesus. Your cross is whatever your source of pain and despair is.

Practice

Today, pray that God shows you how you have the victory. Then tell yourself 17 times that you have the Victory through Jesus Christ.

Day 20

Scripture

Exodus 15:2

The LORD is my strength and song, and he is become my salvation: he is my God, and I will prepare him an habitation; my father's God, and I will.

Thought

When you think of the goodness of God you will see how he has always been there for you, helping you in every aspect. When you think of all he has done for you, you will be able to see how he is worthy of you giving your life to him and his will. There is no one worthy of as much attention. No one else worthy of the praise and devotion, that should be given to God.

Practice

Repeat 5 times, "I give myself away so you can use me." Ask God, how do you need to submit more? Give him the time and space to answer you. When he does, write it down.

Day 21

Scripture

Romans 10:17

So faith comes from hearing, and hearing through the word of Christ.

Thought

Many times people want to gain strength, yet, don't know how. People want to physically get bigger and gain muscle mass and they have to read and research how to do it. Anytime people want to learn more about a topic they research by reading and the more they read the more confidence is gained. If you want to turn your pain into power, you need to read your word. If you really want to expedite the process like an extra fast charger, you can read the word of

God out loud. Listen to his word. Grow your faith through your hearing.

Practice

In your study time, read the word of God out loud. For today and the next 9 days, read your bible aloud when you are reading it.

Day 22

Scripture

Mark 5:36

Overhearing what they had sad, Jesus told him do not be afraid JUST believe.

Thought

When you feed your faith, it will starve your fears. There is a point in your pain you have to take a stand and say this is it and no longer fear. I will stand strong on the word of the Lord, I will not worry. I will speak life and I will see God move in my life and through my life. You will come to a point you will stop looking at your surroundings and just see the goodness of the Lord in your life. No matter how big or small God is blessing you and he has a plan for you. Seeing this will help feed your faith and strengthen your trust in what he is doing in this season of your life. Trust him, stop worrying and fearing, and just believe.

Practice

Pray this prayer, "Dear Lord I magnify your mighty name. Greater is he that is in me than he that is in the world. I repent for my sins and shortcomings. Lord you haven't given me a spirit of fear but of power, love and a sound mind. I have faith in you and I fully trust and believe you. Lord I believe but help me with my unbelief. Fill me with your love and power, help me feed my faith and starve my fears. Have your will in my life and let your promise take root into my inner being. I need your spirit to come and change my pain into power as your word says your strength is made perfect in my weakness. I trust you, I need you, I love you. In Jesus name I pray, Amen."

Day 23

Scripture

Matthew 17:21

But this kind does not go out but through prayer and fasting.

Thought

Prayer and reading the Bible are fundamental disciplines a disciple can do to deepen their relationship with God. Two other disciplines that are less mentioned are, meditating and fasting. Meditating on the word of God will help transform your spiritual life in ways indescribable by words. Fasting will allow you to hear from God and obtain power and direction that surpasses all understanding. It's really unfathomable to the human mind. Fasting can take shape in many forms.

You can fast from food, social media, using certain words, entertainment, and countless of other things. When you fast you are saying, "Lord I want to make room for you, I want to make you priority." Fasting is less about what you are giving up and more about making God a priority. In the times of weakness while fasting, it is important that you put God first and not just give up something for a certain amount of time. Replace whatever you are giving up doing your fast for time with God.

When fasting, you want to make sure you aren't bragging, boasting, or looking as if you are fasting. You also want to put on the whole armor of God on every day of your fast.

Practice

Write down what it is you are fasting for. Truly believe God will reveal to you and move on your behalf. For the Next 7 days fast from either social media or television. The times you would spend doing whichever you give up, replace it by spending time with God. Do one of the four mentioned disciplines. This is going to not only power you but **EMPOWER** you like never before.

***Small testimony I went on a 7 day fast and from that A Painful Purpose was birthed. Yes in 7 days. Give God a try and watch him work. ***

Day 24

Scripture

Nehemiah 8:10

The Joy of the Lord is my strength.

Thought

At times when we hear the word, *Joy*, we may think of happiness. We may think of excitement or any other jubilant emotional state. That is a shallow view of what joy is. Joy isn't predicated upon feelings, moods, or emotions. Joy is a deeper since of peace that lives within you when you are staying connected to the Lord. The reason it is important to have such joy is because it is that deeper relationship with God that supplies you with the strength needed to endure the pain that you experience in this life. God will supply you with joy down deep in your soul. Joy is rooted deep into your being, which holds steadfast where happiness is surface level and will blow away with the force of the wind. God's joy is freeing and releasing.

Practice

Take time today to write a love letter to the Lord. Express how grateful you are for his joy being on, in, and working through your life.

Day 25

Scripture

Matthew 11:28-30

Come to me, all of you who are weary and burdened and I will give you rest.

Thought

When going through life, we experience situations that can really weigh on us and cause us to feel a spiritual heaviness that can have major health ramifications. It's like someone working out trying to lift a large amount of weight on their own. If it's a weight that they aren't used to lifting they may have a bad lifting form and in return they can cause physical harm. When in the weight room and trying to lift heavy loads, it is common knowledge that the one lifting the weight has what is called a spotter.

The spotter helps guide, watch, and at times help lift the weights for the person.

God is the spiritual spotter for the believer. When you have the weight of the world on your shoulders, God is saying, "come to me and give me what is bothering you and I will give you the rest that you need." When you receive rest, you are rejuvenating your spiritual-being to face what life is giving you.

Practice

After reading your scripture and praying take 3 hours to do nothing but rest. Play some Gospel music to set the atmosphere and do nothing but rest. **YOU NEED IT!**

Day 26

Scripture

Proverbs 4:6-7

(6) Do not forsake wisdom, and she will protect you; love her, and she will watch over you. (7) The beginning of wisdom is this: Get wisdom though it cost all you have get understanding.

Thought

Whenever you are going through situations and circumstances and don't understand you can either worry yourself to death trying to figure everything out on your own. Or you can do yesterday's task and give it to God and get rest. If you choose to rest while giving it to God, that is a very important step to gain strength back. Now to really acquire supernatural power from God, you want to learn the lessons that the tester is trying to convey to you through the tests that you experience. The pain can be so heavy that it strips you of everything you have. However, if you keep your faith and ask God for understanding, you will gain a protective, proactive wisdom that if you take care of it, nurture, and grow it, it will protect you from similar situations that are immeasurable.

As you start to gain strength and power back, you want to fence in your God giving power while nurturing and nursing it to levels that you have never experienced before.

Practice

I remember a song by Xscape, named, "Understanding". It stated, "all I need from you is understanding, as simple as 1 2 3 understanding is what I need." The difference from you and Xscape is that you are seeking understanding from God almighty and not man. On a piece of paper ask God for understanding of your top 3 pressing pains. Leave a good amount of space between each of the three pressing needs. Hold on to it as you will need it tomorrow.

Day 27

Scripture

Romans 8:28

God promises to make something good out of the storms that bring devastation to your life.

Thought

God is good on promises and to every promise he makes is yes and Amen. If you think of how the credit scores works, the more you make your payments on time with the right amount, the higher your credit score is the more money someone will lend you. Earlier in the 30 day journey you wrote down how God has come through for you. If he has done it before, he will do it again. How do you know? Because he has great credit, in fact he has a perfect credit score. He always comes through on his word and he is always on time. He has promised to make good out of **EVERYTHING** that you go through in life.

Practice

With the Paper you used yesterday to write the 3 sources of your pain, I want you to write a promise from the bible down under it.

If you need healing write by your stripes I am healed. Do it for each source of your pain. Then pray for supernatural understanding and wisdom for each of the situations.

Day 28

Scripture

Hebrews 13:5

Keep your life free from love of money, and be content with what you have, for he has said, "I will never leave you nor forsake you.

Thought

When going through situations, the devil wants you isolated so he can attack your mind and take you off the course God has for you. If he can make you feel like you are by yourself, he feels he can defeat you because truthfully when we feel all alone we have a feeling of weakness and defeat. He wants to make you feel unworthy or guilty and condemned.

What God wants is to give you assurance and reassurance that he is with you and will always be with you. He loves you and will always love you. He is saying I am with you through everything you have to face in life. He won't leave you and he will not let you go without what you need. A storm with God is better than a storm without him.

Practice

For the next 3 day, fast from food from 7am-6pm. For the time that you normally would eat lunch, spend it meditating on the promises that you wrote under the sources of your pain you feel. Start from Pain 3 today, and tomorrow pain 2, then the last day meditate under the promise for your number one problem. This is setting your relationship with God as a number 1 priority and will allow you to see how he is with you.

Day 29

Scripture

Psalm 55:22

Cast your cares on the Lord and he will sustain you; he will never let the righteous be shaken.

Thought

You will have trials and tribulations in life but God will not let it shake you or break you. You can stand firm on his promises. You can stand firm on his word. You can stand in the midst of whatever you are going through because he is your strength and he is your provider.

Practice

Let this phrase ring in your spirit throughout the day, "I can stand through it all with God by my side."

Day 30

Scripture

James 1:2-4

My brothers, count it all joy when you face trials of many kinds, because you know that the testing of your faith develops perseverance. Perseverance must finish its work so that you may be mature and complete not lacking anything.

Thought

When you face trials and experience pain it is to make you stronger. *What doesn't kill you makes you stronger.* It is designed to elevate you spiritually. It is to give you what it is that you need. God designed the pain to strengthen you as long as you endure you will experience a growth and power to take you to the next level in life.

Practice

Today, pray giving thanks to God for your pain and declare that the pain has strengthened you and given you power like no other.

4-U-Nique Publishing

Read excerpts, get exclusive inside looks at exciting new titles and authors, find tour schedules and enter contests.

www.4-U-NiquePublishing.com

Need help publishing your masterpiece? We are happy to help.

Email us at info@4-U-NiquePublishing.com

Made in the USA
San Bernardino, CA
21 January 2020